CAFE RACERS
of the 1970s

Previous page:
1977 Rickman-Kawasaki CR
(was that for café racer?).

Above: A 1973 Dunstall-Norton 850. Just one of the many café racers built by the famous customising house during the decade.

CAFE RACERS
of the 1970s

MACHINES,
RIDERS AND LIFESTYLE
A PICTORIAL REVIEW

Mick Walker

The Crowood Press

First published in Great Britain as
Superbike Specials of the 1970s
in 1994 by Windrow & Greene

This edition published in 2011 by
The Crowood Press Ltd
Ramsbury, Marlborough
Wiltshire SN8 2HR

www.crowood.com

**British Library Cataloguing in
Publication Data**
A catalogue record for this book is
available from the British Library.

ISBN 978 1 84797 283 5

Typeset by ghk DESIGN,
Chiswick, London

Printed and bound in Singapore by
Craft Print International Ltd

ACKNOWLEDGEMENTS

In retrospect, the 1970s was a good time to have been alive — at least from a motorcycling perspective. Not even the energy crisis of 1974 affected a decade in which motorcycling boomed as it had not done since the immediate postwar period.

During the decade a wondrous array of motorcycles — Café racers — appeared in a continuous stream, both from the world's major factories and (of more significance to this book) from a number of specialist sources. Some of these, such as Dunstall, Rickman and Seeley, were already household names. Others, such as Bimota, Van Veen and Magni, were at the outset of the decade no more than dreams in the minds of their would-be creators.

In assembling the material for Café Racers of the 1970s, I have been fortunate to have not only my own memories of life in the motorcycle industry during that time to draw on, but also those of the many, many friends I made along the way, who have been only too pleased to relive and share their experiences. It would be an almost impossible task to list everyone who helped with this book, so if your name does not appear please forgive the omission and accept my heartfelt thanks:
the late Ken Cobbing, Keith Davies, Dave Degens, Paul Dunstall, John Fernley, Luigi Giacometti, Doug Jackson, Dave Kay, Alan Kimber, Arturo Magni, Tim Parker, Don and Derek Rickman, Colin Seeley, Phil Todd, the late Don Upshaw.

The photographs are mainly from my personal collection, but some of the above-named also helped in this area, for which I am grateful.

Finally I would like to thank Bryan Kennedy of Windrow & Greene, together with my old friend Robin Read, for making this book happen.

Mick Walker
Wisbech, Cambridgeshire.

Contents

Opposite page: Dunstall GS1000. *Motor Cycle News* tested one at 156mpg in 1979.

Below: Turbocharged Kawasaki 1-litre four turning on the power at the drag strip, circa 1977.

ORIGINS

In many ways the Café Racer of the 1970s was a direct follow-on to the Café Racer of the previous decade. In the USA, however, the two were almost the same, as the American café racer craze was itself a phenomenon of the 1970s.

Typical of the early café racer were the Rickman Enfield and Dunstall Norton, each in its own way the last of a particular breed of motorcycle. By 1972, the entire scene was changing. The CB750 Honda, T500 Suzuki and H2 Kawasaki had appeared, while the Z1 was imminent.

On the race-circuits, the TD and TR Yamaha twins were dominant, whilst the four-strokes were hanging on by a thread in the larger-capacity classes. An an example, Ducati won the inaugural Imola 200 in April 1972, but a year later the two-stroke had almost completely taken over.

As far as the roadgoing public was concerned, motorcycling had spent a decade in the doldrums — which was why many had chosen to build what *they* wanted, in the shape of the myriad café racers, rather than accept what manufacturers had offered. But as the decade progressed, sales of motorcycles increased with dramatic speed. In this new era of refined four-cylinder models, with push-button starting and other rider-friendly innovations, the Enfield and Norton twins were obsolete at a stroke, losing their appeal to all but a small clique of tradition-oriented enthusiasts. Thus was the stage set for a new wave of exotica, both from the manufacturers *and* from the specialists who are the subject of this book. The 1970s was to see a frantic race to create ever-more powerful machinery, and many of the motorcycle world's all-time greats appeared during this decade.

Just stop and consider. From Japan: Honda Gold Wing and CBX six; Kawasaki Z1 and Z1300 six; Suzuki GT750 and GS750/1000; Yamaha XS750/850. From Italy: Ducati 750/900SS, Mike Hailwood Replica; Moto Guzzi V7 Sport and Le Mans; Laverda SFC and Jota; Benelli 750/900Sei. From Germany: BMW R90S. The list is impressive.

One would have thought that against the might of the series production manufacturers, with such a formidable array of engineering skills and model ranges, the limited-production specialist bike-builders and customisers would have stood no chance. But, for a variety of reasons, such was not the case.

For a start, there were then, as there have always been, those who desired to own something truly unique. Then there was the saga of the Japanese Superbikes which didn't handle, while the Italian industry shot itself in the foot by producing some truly superb bikes which had truly awful finishes. And, finally, there was the fact that the major manufacturers always had to keep one eye on the increasingly vociferous 'green' lobby, with the result that, as the decade

Opposite page

Above: As the 1970s dawned the British were hanging on, just, to their dominance of the big-bike market. Like Paul Dunstall, Ian Kennedy was a man who had succeeded in the 1960s with a range of tasty café racers. During the 1960s, he worked closely with the Rhodesian racer-engineer, Colin Lyster, mainly offering tuned and customised Norton twins. One of Kennedy's final efforts was this 750 Commando with the usual café racer credentials plus a twin disc brake conversion up front.

Below: Yet more café racer-inspired iron, in the shape of these Dark Star and Road Star BSA B50-based machines. Dealer-conceived, these had excellent specification and finish, but never went beyond the prototype stage. Quite simply, the unit construction singles lacked the aura of the sadly missed Clubman's Gold Star.

Above: Dutchman Gerhard Klomps sets off on the maiden test of the prototype Van Veen Wankel in November 1972. Unlike the production OCR1000 model, this first machine used a Japanese Mazda RX2 car engine in a Moto Guzzi V7 chassis.

progressed, many machines became overloaded with environmental features. (The Ducati V-twin is a good illustration of this trend.)

In summary, the 1970s was very much the era of the factory-built Superbikes which didn't always perform as their manufacturers promised and their customers would have liked, be it from a strictly performance viewpoint, or from that of handling, braking, or less-than-perfect ancillary equipment or finish. This in turn created a decade of *specialist* Superbikes, which resolved one or more of the problems outlined above on a single machine. Among the plethora of names which flourished in this environment, and which this book will look at more closely, were Dunstall, Gus Kuhn, Seeley, Rickman, Bimota, Magni, Dresda, Münch and Van Veen.

There were others, too, some of whom produced just a single prototype, others a handful, and yet more (Moto Martin, Harris, Niko Bakker, Moko, Hesketh *et al.*) whose achievements belong to the 1980s.

The 1970s also saw many riders forsake their 'pudding basin' helmet and goggles for the 'Ned Kelly' full-face type with its integral visor, and witnessed the widespread use of leathers, either separate jacket and jeans or one-piece racing type.

Below: In October 1973 the Norton factory created their own café racer with the John Player Norton street bike, based on the Commando but equipped with an eye-catching fairing and matching seat and tail unit. It was offered with either the normal 829cc engine, as used in the other models that year, or, for competition purposes, a short-stroke 750. This machine retained the big twin's 77mm bore, but had the stroke reduced to 80.4mm to give a capacity of 749cc.

Above: Aftermarket exhaust systems were a strong feature of the 1970s. Pictured here is just a small selection, including examples for Kawasaki Triples, Z1, Honda CB750, Norton Commando and Triumph Twin. Generally, they were much cheaper than standard, but much noisier.

Above: The Honda CB400F Four was a classic of its kind — a Superbike in miniature. Many dealers and specialists offered customised versions. One of the best was this Dixon Racing example, with 460cc big bore kit, matt black exhaust system, light alloy wheel rims, Dunlop TT100 tyres, S&W rear shocks, nose fairing with choice of tinted or clear screen, and metalflake gold-green finish. Year is 1976.

Tyres and other accessories were another vital development area of the decade. With such vast increases in power output, it became imperative to update the type and size of rubber being put down on the road. To meet the demand, Dunlop introduced the TT100 and later the Arrowmax, Avon the Roadrunner, and Pirelli the Phantom.

Another important advance was the introduction of the 'O' ring chain, which gave considerably longer life than the old unprotected-link variety of earlier days.

With each passing year, tyres grew slicker and wider, while finaldrive chains also grew in size in an attempt to keep up with engine power output figures.

Yet another development was rider protection in the shape of fairings. During the decade several major manufacturers, including Norton, Ducati, Moto Guzzi and BMW, provided at least some of their standard production models with a degree of streamlining.

As standard exhaust systems became more restrictive (and much more expensive), so another cottage industry boomed: the production and sale of a vast array of aftermarket systems. Unfortunately, many of these were both ultra-noisy and of inferior quality. But there were exceptions, such as the superb Motad range.

For most of the 1970s, the motorcycle trade at all levels saw sales rise with each succeeding year. Sales of new motorcycles in Britain increased from less than 90,000 at the start of the decade to some 350,000 at its close. But, as if to prove the adage that what goes up must

Above: This neatly styled Dunstall-Suzuki GT550 also dates from 1976. It was sold through the official UK importer's dealer network with full warranty. The GT750 watercooled model was also available with the Dunstall treatment.

come down, the 1980s were to witness one of the worst recessions the industry had known. Dealerships, some built up over many years, disappeared almost overnight, affecting both distributors and manufacturers. The larger ones with more backing were able to survive; but many—including some of the specialist café racer builders—lacked the resources to ride out the storm and were were lost to the motorcycling world for ever.

Yet, amazingly, some of the newer concerns, notably Bimota and Magni, were to survive and become famous in their own right against a backdrop which included the arrival of a new breed of race-replicas with phenomenal power, superb handling and brick-wall braking qualities... But that is another story, perhaps for another book.

Left: Many owners created their own dream machines. This is someone's ultimate Ducati 900SS. Modifications include two-into-one exhaust, massive alloy tank, single seat, home-made front mudguard and rearsets, alloy rims without the usual water-collecting 'wells', half fairing and many other unique features. Everything has been drilled and lightened, and there are perspex covers to show off the bevel gears.

Below: This very special Laverda Jota was built by Avon Bikes of Bristol from a frame and bodywork supplied by the Italian Motoplast company during the 1970s. Other Laverda specials came from Egli, Slater Brothers, Harris, Cropredy (Liberator), Motodd, Spondon, Saxon, Difazio, and Mead & Tomkinson (Nessie). Untuned, the 981cc (75x74mm) dohc, transverse, three-cylinder engine was capable of 90bhp at 7,600rpm. In 1976 *Motor Cycle* recorded a best one-way speed of 140.04mph, making it the fastest machine tested by the magazine that year.

DUNSTALL

Paul Dunstall entered the 1970s renowned as 'King of the customisers' and as the man more responsible than any other for the café racer boom of the previous decade.

Dunstall had displayed a talent for judging exactly what the market needed; but during the 1970s, despite the appearance of some truly remarkable machinery bearing his name, this magic touch was not always in evidence.

He stuck with Norton for a shade too long, and when he finally switched to Japanese machinery the styling was not always right. But even so, the Paul Dunstall Organisation was still a major force in customising and aftermarket goodies. And, of course, with its complete Dunstall motorcycles which, in the cases of Kawasaki and Suzuki, had full factory backing.

Dunstall also played a leading role in the transfer of the café racer craze to the United States. By the middle of the 1970s he was able to boast a widespread dealer network in North America, backed up by the very comprehensive 60-page Dunstall Power Catalogue.

Although later in the decade he was responsible for producing the classic Dunstall Suzuki GS1000 café racer, Paul Dunstall, like many others, became a victim of the sharp decline in the motorcycle market at the end of the 1970s, with its attendant drop in sales and profits. He commented recently: 'I'd been spoilt by the buoyant market for years. But it was becoming a bore, with accountants peering over your shoulder' — a familiar lament from those led by enthusiasm rather than hunger for business success.

Dunstall leased out unused factory space to other businesses and finally sold the Dunstall name in 1982. It died within three years. Dunstall has since been running property companies from his home in Shoreham, Kent.

Right: The man himself with the latest Dunstall Norton Commando Export in February 1970. In the author's opinion, this marked a highpoint in Dunstall development, with excellent styling and a comprehensive range of equipment which included a dual-disc kit, exhaust systems, glassfibre ware and performance tuning. There was even a Quaife six-speed gearbox option.

Above: Machines being assembled at Dunstall's new factory on the Greater London Council's industrial estate at Thamesmead, built on reclaimed marshland on the south bank of the Thames. The company began operations in the spring of 1970. In the mid-1970s, it moved once again — this time to Crabtree Manorway, Belvedere, Kent.

Below: Dunstall Commando with full fairing, double-disc front brake (original type), wrap-around front mudguard, dual racing seat, alloy rims, clip-ons, rearsets, Dunstall Decibel megaphone silencers, fork gaiters and quick-action filler cap. At its peak, the company built more than 750 Dunstall Nortons in a single year.

Left: Testing an 810cc Dunstall Commando in early 1971 — note black tyre marks on the road. Pudding-basin helmet and Barbour jacket were still in fashion. Dunstall Commandos all had race-proved cylinder head modification to accommodate a 1⅝" inlet valve, in place of the standard 1½" component. The valve angle was steepened by 1½ degrees and the combustion chamber reshaped.

Ports and inlet manifolds were opened out and polished, and special valves in H18S steel wire used with dual-rate springs and bronze-dural guides. Amal 32mm Concentrics replaced the original 30mm instruments and compression was raised to 10 or 10.5:1, depending on customer requirements. Lucas capacitor ignition was used. These modifications increased power from 50 to 67bhp at 7,000rpm.

Opposite page: Designed by Eddie Robinson, who was responsible for the Dunstall racing spine frame, this twin-disc front brake was introduced for the 1970 season and differed in three respects from the earlier Dunstall twin front disc kit.

Housings, cast integrally with each fork leg, contained the pads which gripped on stainless steel discs, rigidly attached to the wheel hub instead of floating.

Three assemblies were available — for BSA and Triumph forks from 1969 onwards, for Norton from 1964 onward (shown), and for pre-1964 Nortons. In addition, Phil Read used the system on his 1971 250cc World Championship-winning Yamaha.

Each assembly comprised two cast-aluminium fork legs and integral calipers, light-alloy hub and bolted-on discs, a Lockheed magnesium master cylinder and integral lever for handlebar mounting and high-pressure flexible hoses.

In appearance, the 1970 Dunstall brake had none of the 'bittiness' of the previous bolt-on discs, and workmanship and general finish were superb. The one element open to question was the use of stainless steel for the discs. Although it eliminated the one big drawback of ordinary steel discs — that they rusted after rain — it could not provide the same extra-sure grip in wet conditions.

Left: The 1971 Dunstall Norton Sprint model was offered in three basic guises: the Tourer, Sprint (shown), and Export. Besides the engine modifications already outlined, all 1971 Dunstall Nortons had, as standard, optional 2½- or four-gallon glassfibre or 3½-gallon light-alloy tank, GT dual seat and glassfibre or polished light-alloy front mudguard.

It is impossible to pinpoint the full specification of the Tourer, Sprint or Export models, as Dunstall was prepared to ring the changes to suit individual requirements. Both Tourer and Sprint were supplied as standard, with a twin leading shoe drum front brake. The Dunstall twin-disc unit (shown) was an extra-cost option, though standard fitment on the Export.

The Tourer was also available with Craven panniers and luggage rack, and all three versions came with a lockable compartment in the rear of the seat which provided useful space for items such as tools, plugs and light-bulbs.

Above: Another Dunstall Norton which was new for 1971 was the 810 model. This was available either as a complete motorcycle or a separate kit. Tested by *Motor Cycle* on March 3 1971, the larger-bore model knocked .4 of a second off the already good standing quarter-mile figure of 12.3, achieving 11.9 seconds. Maximum speed had increased to 131mph.

Opposite page, bottom: A notable Dunstall Norton 'extra' for the 1971 season was the two-into-one exhaust system, designed by Dr Gordon Blair, which gave a useful boost to performance. Blair's system was developed from an earlier layout which he had designed for cars. Using his computer facilities at Queen's University, Belfast, he had found a way of improving acceleration and top speed, without affecting fuel consumption. The system was claimed to harness the resonances in the single pipe, which passed beneath the power unit and then branched out into two again, with a silencer on each side of the rear wheel.
With standard Norton exhaust, the 1971 Dunstall Commando was capable of 120mph and could cover the quarter-mile sprint in 13.5 seconds — a terminal speed of 100mph. Fitted with the combination of Blair exhaust pipes and Dunstall Decibel Silencers, the figures increased to 125mph, 12.3 seconds and 104mph.

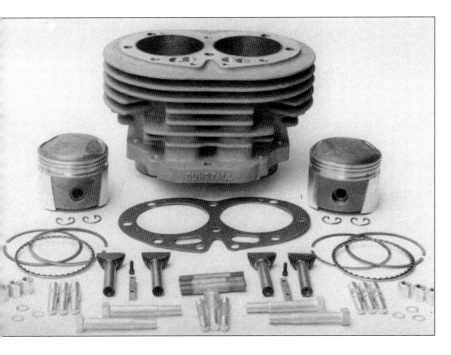

Left: Dunstall 810cc cylinder kit for Norton Commando. The 1973 version illustrated here had undergone considerable improvement, including a new type liner and bottom tappet location, together with new base nuts. The kit consisted of a light-alloy cylinder block, with spun-cast liners, new pistons — claimed to be the same weight as Dunstall's 750cc type — and cam followers which were only half the weight of the standard ones, plus retaining studs, nuts and gaskets. The block, which had 76mm bores (compared with 73mm standard) was half the weight of the original Norton component — 4.5kg (10lbs) against 9kg (20lbs) — and fitted without modification to the existing head or crankshaft mouth.

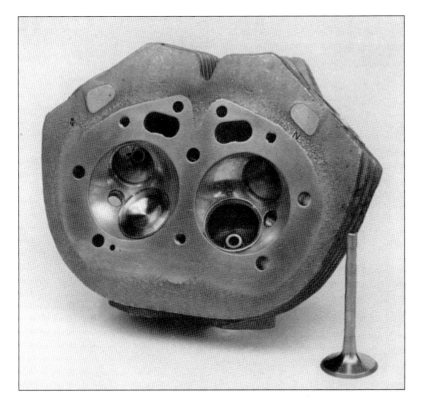

Left: 1973 also saw this improved 'Dunstallised' Norton cylinder head. It had been modified as follows: re-sphered combustion chambers from 68mm to 73mm; steeper inlet valve angle $26\frac{1}{2}$ degrees instead of 28 degrees; larger inlet valves, $1\frac{5}{8}$" in place of $1\frac{1}{2}$"; larger inlet ports, $1\frac{1}{4}$" instead of 13/16"; inlet and exhaust ports reshaped and polished for maximum gas flow; bronze inlet valve seats. Combined, these modifications added between 4 and 5bhp by increasing the efficiency of the engine and allowed the head to pass more fuel-air mixture. The modified head came complete with a pair of new $1\frac{5}{8}$" inlet valves.

Above: Paul Dunstall's switch from British to Japanese machinery was slow, although he did build this prototype Kawasaki 500 three-cylinder two-stroke-engined racing machine in 1970. Later that year, it was also announced that in 1971 he would be offering a Dunstall-modified Honda CB750 Four Super Sports Roadster. The machine was equipped with a modified cylinder head, reshaped and polished ports, 10:1 compression ratio (9:1 standard), light-alloy rims, Dunlop K81 tyres, 3½-gallon glassfibre tank, GT dual seat (with locking tail compartment) and 'Ace'-style handlebars. This followed a one-off order for a prototype machine by Zachary Reynolds — part owner of the Reynolds Tobacco Company, makers of Camel cigarettes — who kept an impressive collection of 50 high-performance motorcycles at his home in Winston Salem, North Carolina.

Above: Another four-cylinder Dunstall-Honda roadburner was this smaller 500-engined version which first appeared early in 1973. Specification included alloy wheel rims, Dunlop TT100 tyres, glassfibre front mudguard, GT fairing, clip-on handlebars, chrome fork covers, five-gallon fuel tank (alloy for UK market), special side panels, GT dual seat, Girling rear shocks, rearset footrest kit, Dunstall Power Exhaust System and Dunstall Decibel silencers. Selected engine tuning was also available.

Opposite page

Above: Special Dunstall high-compression pistons for the Honda CB750. These were manufactured from low-expansion, high-silicon content, stanifont material, spun-cast for maximum strength. The 10.25:1 compression ratio improved the engine's efficiency, giving better acceleration and higher top speed. The complete set of four, including piston rings, gudgeon pins and circlips, sold for £17.00.

Below: Dunstall-Honda clip-ons were a unique design which fitted on to the fork top nuts and front pinch bolts. Slotted and drilled to take the stock controls and cables and supplied complete with light-alloy fork top nuts, securing bolts and pinch bolts, they were available for 500, 750 and 889cc models. Note use of stock Nippondenso clocks and 'idiot' light console.

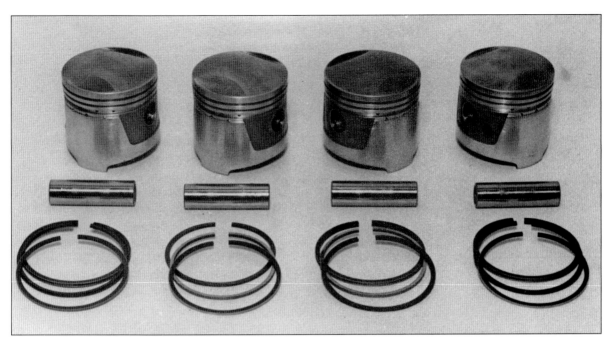

Left: Another Dunstall-Honda accessory was this rearset footrest kit, designed specifically for use with the Dunstall clip-ons. It provided the combination of footrests, gear lever and brake pedal mounted in a position which was best suited to the clip-on handlebars. Again, it was suitable for all three Dunstall-Honda four-cylinder models.

Below, left: Derived from the earlier Dunstall Power Exhaust System used on the Dunstall-Norton Commando range, the Honda version retained the original's feature of specially coupled pipes to take full advantage of opposing pressure waves and use them to improve the engine's efficiency. After exhaustive analysis, these coupled systems proved to be most efficient, giving a .6 second improvement on the standing quarter and an extra 5mph on top speed. When supplied as a separate kit, the system came complete with a set of exhaust pipes, a pair of Dunstall Decibel Silencers and all fixing brackets and clamps.

Opposite page: The American magazine *Motorcyclist* called it the 'Zee Whizz': the Dunstall-Kawasaki 1100 with 88bhp on tap.

The Dunstall concept was basically a 'drop-on': the glassfibre tank cover slipped over the original tank which was retained in its entirety, although the stock Kawasaki saddle and rear mudguards were replaced with Dunstall saddle and 'glass, together with clip-ons and rearsets. The basic frame and chassis were unchanged except for Borrani alloy rims laced to Kawasaki hubs, and Dunlop TT100 rubber. Also featured were four-into-two Dunstall silencers, café racer fairing and front mudguard, rearsets with passenger peg brackets and pegs, dual front discs, swivel-type Stadium mirror and monogrammed grips. All electrics, instrumentation and switchgear were stock Kawasaki.

Not just a larger bore, the engine featured thick-sleeved barrels and flowed heads. And, as though performance was not enough, cylinder and head exteriors were superbly detailed with what appeared to be a baked-on, satin-smooth porcelain finish. Black barrels and yellow heads were colour coded to match the professional 'glass work above, giving an impressively well-integrated effect.

Below: The 1975 Dunstall-
Honda CB750 (left) and
Dunstall-Kawasaki 1100.
An American advertisement of
the time proclaimed, 'Paul
Dunstall didn't jump on the
Café Racer bandwagon — he's
been driving it for fifteen years!'

Opposite page: The Suzuki Dunstall GT750 was the result of an
agreement reached between Paul Dunstall and the British Suzuki
importers for the 1976 season. Available in racing or touring style,
the 739cc (70x64mm) three-cylinder piston port two-stroke bore the
advantage of a full Suzuki factory-backed guarantee. Advertising
listed all the benefits of the Dunstall package.

Overleaf: Probably Dunstall's finest machine of the 1970s, the
superb 997cc (70x64.8mm) Dunstall-Suzuki GS1000, which
Motorcycle News tested at 156mph (Dunstall claimed 144mph).
Its red, yellow and black finish ensured that it stood out from the
crowd, even when stationary. Its specification included 29mm
carburettors, modified cylinder head with reshaped and enlarged
ports, 10.5:1 compression ratio, Dunstall Power Exhaust System,
Dunstall Deluxe Silencer, Super Sports fairing in Heron-Suzuki race
replica colours (as were the special seat and front mudguard), Super
Sports handlebars ('Ace'-type bars, not clip-ons), rearset footrest kit
and controls, 48-tooth rear wheel sprocket to raise gearing, and a
dry weight of 223kg (4921lbs). It could cover the quarter-mile in 11.4
seconds. A 750 version was also available. Reproduced here is the
centrefold from the very rare GS1000/750 sale brochure.

An exciting new development by Suzuki GB and Paul Dunstall — the Suzuki Dunstall GT750

Available in two forms: Racing-style/ Touring-style. New 1976 Suzuki GT750s can be supplied complete, and a Suzuki Dunstall GT750 kit to fit all previous GT750s will be shortly available, in both forms.

The equipment comprises: Suzuki Dunstall one-piece fuel tank cover and dual racing seat, with rear number plate and rear light mounting, handlebar fairing with tinted windscreen, all edging material and special handlebars, plus sports front mudguard.

All glassfibre items are colour pigmented and finished in high gloss; metal fittings are plated.

Optional extras include: Mag alloy wheels and special exhaust system (available in 1976).

SUZUKI GB

87 Beddington Lane, Croydon, Surrey CRO 4TD.

Designed & Produced by Maurice Spalding Publicity, London SE6 2JT.

Dunstall Suzu

The ultimate super bikes, in a class of their own. They provide
output, outstanding performance and superb handling.

With a top speed in excess of 145 M.P.H. (135 M.P.H. for the 7
production bikes on the road. Even more impressive is the incredi
the S.S. Quarter Mile in a record time of only 11.4 seconds (12.4 se

This unparalleled performance is achieved through higher effic
ports, higher compression ratio, a tuned exhaust and careful
'hand built' assembly gives smooth, controlled power from
1,000 r.p.m. right up to red line.

This shattering performance would be wasted without
brakes to match, but with twin disc brakes at the front and
another disc at the rear the stopping power is a match for the
performance.

To fully
utilise this
performance a rider needs
to be in complete control. The careful combination
of footrest positioning, handlebar angle, low seat height and low
drag fairing enables the rider to get comfortable and be in comple

GS1000/750

fect combination of high power

ey are quite simply the fastest
eleration. The 1000cc model covers
for the 750).

arge bore carburettors, hand finished

Performance figures independently and
electronically timed by the N.S.A.
for total accuracy.

DUNSTALL GS 1000

Maximum Speed   144 m.p.h.
(Average speed for Flying ¼ mile)

S.S. Quarter Mile 11.5 seconds

Our own electronically timed
figures for the

DUNSTALL GS 750

Maximum speed   135 m.p.h.

S.S. Quarter Mile 12.4 seconds

trol.

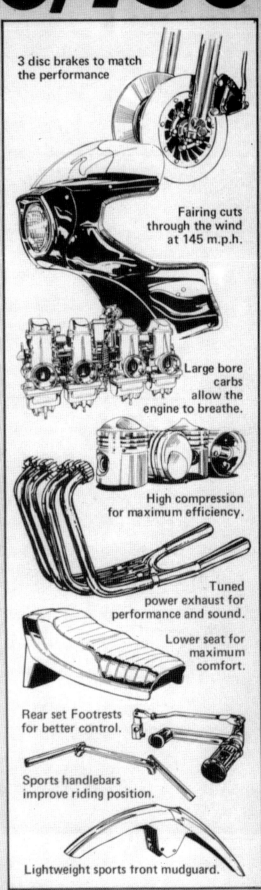

3 disc brakes to match
the performance

Fairing cuts
through the wind
at 145 m.p.h.

Large bore
carbs
allow the
engine to breathe.

High compression
for maximum efficiency.

Tuned
power exhaust for
performance and sound.

Lower seat for
maximum
comfort.

Rear set Footrests
for better control.

Sports handlebars
improve riding position.

Lightweight sports front mudguard.

READ TITAN

Opposite page:
A Read Kawasaki Titan Mach III in half fairing. All the glassfibre ware was manufactured by Churchgate Mouldings. Performance was basically unchanged from the standard roadster.

Right:
The 1972 version of the Read Kawasaki Titan Mach III. The separate parts included full fairing, top fairing, tank and single seat or touring tank with standard dual seat, abbreviated alloy sports front mudguard, alloy wheel rims, Girling or Koni rear suspension units, rear sets, clip-ons and front crash bars. The complete motorcycle, in sports trim, sold for £760.

The famous customising house of Read Titan was one of the first to cater for the new breed of high-performance, large-capacity Japanese motorcycles which hit Britain in the late 1960s and early 1970s.

Whilst others (notably Paul Dunstall, Eddie Dow and Ian Kennedy) found the transition from 1960s British to 1970s Japanese difficult to handle, Read Titan found the change simpler.

Based in Leytonstone, East London, the company targeted Honda and Kawasaki with considerable effect. Their major efforts were directed towards the 750 Honda four and 500 Kawasaki triple, though customers could also order other machines in both marques' line-ups or the separate component parts for their own machinery.

Unlike Rickman and Dresda, for example, Read Titan did not build their own frames; nor did they carry out extensive 'in-house' engine work. But they did offer a range of goodies to tempt buyers, much the same as many a specialist dealer had done so successfully with the café racer crowd of the 1960s.

Overleaf: The Read Titan stand at the 1974 London-based Racing and Sporting Show with a line-up of customised Hondas: from left, CB750, CB500/4 and CB250. The biggest Honda (named the Daytona) was very much the jewel in the Read Titan crown. In the background are some of the vast array of bolt-on goodies for various Honda and Kawasaki models offered by the company.

Left: Three years later and Read Titan had gone one hundred percent Honda. Typical of their offerings at this time was this very tasty CB400F café racer.

Below: Official Honda Great Britain glamour girl Dinah May poses with the simply awful (to this writer's eyes) Read Titan Sabre. This ugly creation marked a low point in the customising giant's output. Underneath that massive fairing tank and seat is one of the 1977 CB750F2 Hondas. Other visible changes include the cast alloy wheels (which replaced Honda's Comstar components) and the rear-set footrests.

RICKMAN

Following its great successes in the 1960s, Rickman Engineering concentrated its energies from 1970 to 1974 on the production of lightweight motocross machines. More than 12,000 were sold, mainly to the USA. In addition, several British police forces looked to the New Milton, Hampshire factory for better-handling motorcycles for fast patrol work. A special-purpose police bike was designed, incorporating all the qualities for which Rickman had become world-famous.

It not only used a Metisse frame but also Rickman forks and disc brakes and was fully equipped with custom-built glassfibre panniers, fairing and side-moulding — and a blue light.

By 1973 the Rickman Police Triumph had won favour with several forces and was to be seen in daily use throughout large areas of the British Isles. There was also a lightweight police mount, powered by a German 125 Zündapp two-stroke motor.

Of the total factory output in 1974, some 90 percent was exported to North America. This million pounds-worth of orders won the company the Queen's Award to Industry. In the same year, however, the BSA/Triumph group finally folded and the contract to build motocross machines for the USA was not renewed.

This left Rickman with the weighty problem of how to utilise their factory and staff. With few options open to them, the board decided to develop the Superbike concept, giving it the designating letters CR — for Competition Replica, or was it Café Racer? The company also found it necessary to develop a range of accessories to complement their established glassfibre production.

Natural progression expanded the range to suit new Japanese motorcycles, and production of the CR chassis kits built up to around 60 per month while fairing production alone grew from around 50 units in 1973 to 12,000 by 1977.

Not long afterwards, though, the market slumped and Rickman looked towards general engineering to keep itself alive and occupied.

Right: The Rickman brothers (Derek, left, and Don) had a dream of manufacturing complete machines, including engines; but the closest they came to it was production of their eight-valve Triumph conversion kit, an earlier 500cc conversion kit for the BSA Victor, and the ill-fated Read Weslake Metisse racer. Plus, of course, a series of Rickman-framed machines with a variety of engines including AJS 7R and Matchless G50, Royal Enfield Interceptor, 750 Honda and 900/1000 Kawasakis.

Above: The Read Weslake Metisse was a disappointment to all
involved. It first appeared with Phil Read in the saddle at the North
West 200 in Ireland during May 1969, covering only a short distance
before oiling problems caused its retirement. Its next public outing
was not for another *28 months*, when Martin Ashwood put it through
its paces at an open practice session at Silverstone in August 1971.
In the interim, the Weslake concern had drastically modified the
engine, although it retained the original 75.4x56.7mm (496cc) engine
size. The crank throws had been altered from 360 to 180 degrees,
the oiling system totally redesigned and the bottom end beefed up.
In addition, Weslake's technical director, Mike Daniels, announced
that the original five-speed gearbox internals had been replaced by
a Rod Quaife cluster.
Power at the crankshaft was reported to have been over 75bhp.
Normal rev limit was 11,000rpm, but on test runs the engines had
occasionally been taken up to 13,000.
Later in 1971 the Read Weslake Metisse was raced at Brands by
Ashwood, but after a poor start was retired with ignition problems.
Following yet more testing, the project was finally abandoned: oil
temperature proved an insurmountable problem, even with a large
cooler fitted. A sad end to a machine from which many had expected
so much.

Below: Another co-operation which would ultimately fail (though for different reasons from the Weslake debacle) was the Rickman Enfield. The Rickman brothers became involved with the Enfield marque in 1969, and the first result was a Rickman Metisse fitted with one of the Interceptor Mark II engines. Its first public showing was at the Sporting and Racing Show in January 1970. The combination of the, and reliable 736cc (71x93mm) ohv engine with the superb Metisse chassis produced a generally excellent machine which, with less weight than the standard Enfield, was capable of between 115 and 118mph. The frame was of all-welded construction with duplex tubes throughout and was finished, as was the Rickman practice, in bright nickel plating. The swinging arm was mounted on an eccentric

pivot to provide a more reliable method of rear chain adjustment and the front forks were of the well-known Rickman road racing pattern. Both hubs carried Lockheed hydraulically operated single-disc brakes — unusual at that time on road-going machines. A few sported a front disc, but virtually none had discs at both ends. The tank, seat and mudguarding were manufactured in glassfibre. The dual ignition coils nestled just aft of the Albion gearbox, with the area over them boxed in for battery and tools. One of the more controversial features was the method of mounting the rider's footrests: each was clamped into a small vertically-mounted tube welded to the outer side of its respective exhaust pipe. Odd as it might have appeared, this system apparently functioned without fuss or bother.

Above: The Series II Interceptor engine used in the Rickman Enfield had first appeared late in 1968. Although based around the old Series I assembly, it had undergone several important modifications, the most notable of these being to the lubrication system.

In the Series II engine there was a true wet sump system equipped with a single oil-pump. Thus the oil was contained in a new ribbed section at the base of the crankshaft assembly. There was also a totally new timing cover with the rear half of the old pump drive shaft. The oil pump itself fitted into the rear of this cover, rather than being tucked out of sight, and the oil supply was 60psi to the big-ends and 15psi to the valve gear. The lubricant drained back to the sump by gravitational force; there was a fine-mesh gauze filter to protect the pump, while the traditional Enfield felt filter and its magnet were relocated from the timing cover to a vertical housing behind the cylinders.

The new timing cover was of triangular shape

Below: Combination of Rickman Norton-type front forks and efficient Lockheed hydraulically operated front disc brake, used on various street and racing Metisse models for almost a decade.

and was no longer extended back for a magneto drive. Instead, there was Lucas capacitor ignition, triggered by contact points opened by a cam on the end of the exhaust cam.

The contact points were housed in the timing cover with a small casting over them, while the nearside end of the exhaust cam drove the tacho. Twin Amal concentric carbs, an 8.5:1 compression and duplex primary chain were part of the specification. There was also a revised clutch, together with several other smaller and

less significant changes over the Mark I.
On the Rickman version, customers gained a comprehensive air cleaner, oil cooler, sump guard and seat rail — all at no added cost, except on the first batch of bikes where these components were extra-cost options.

Marketing of the Rickman Enfield was handled by Elite Motors of Tooting, south London. Sales were eventually brought to a halt by the closure of the Enfield works, an event which in no way tarnished the excellence of the Rickman project.

Below: After the Rickman Enfield came another British-engined Metisse chassis — the three-cylinder (67x70mm) Triumph Trident-powered machine shown here. Available for either road or track use, only a small number were made, as by this time Triumph, like Enfield, had hit trouble, with the collapse of the BSA empire. The version shown was for competition only. Specification included an F750 engine, three-into-one exhaust, Girling rear shocks, oil cooler and alloy tanks, plus other customary Rickman features.

Opposite page

Above: The Luton-based RGM dealership was a leading Rickman dealer in the early 1970s. Seen on the far left of this shot is John Judge, who headed the dealership, with two Rickman Tridents and potential customers. Both machines have Churchgate fairings and race-type specifications. Following the formation of the NVT (Norton Villiers Triumph) rescue package in 1973, both T150 and T160 engines were used. Both were good for more than 130mph.

Below: The first Japanese-powered Rickman Superbike, the CR750. Specification included new or renovated 736.5cc (61x63mm) Honda CB750 sohc four-cylinder engine, Rickman chassis kit and bodywork, Rickman forks and front wheel, Girling (or similar) rear shocks. The standard package used the stock exhaust, electrics and instrumentation; but some bikes appeared with custom paint finish, Piper four-into-one sports/racing exhaust and engine tuning.

A 1974 photograph of two Rickmans doing battle on an airfield strip. Left, a unit construction 649cc Triumph Bonneville-Metisse; right, a Honda CR750 Metisse. History does not record the outcome of this particular battle.

Below: Next in line for the Rickman treatment came the fabulous 903cc (66x66mm) Z1 Kawasaki, dubbed 'King of the Road' early in its career. The year is 1975, by which time Kawasaki's latest was the Z1B.

The Z1 series enjoyed rave reviews from the world's press and they were fully deserved — though it has to be said that its handling and roadholding left something to be desired. Rehoused in the race-breed Rickman Metisse chassis, the machines' 130mph+ capacity could be used to better advantage.

Opposite page, bottom: The Rickman Kawasaki could be ordered in various guises, but the café racer shown here was the most popular.
The Rickman CR café racer turned a stock Z1 into a sleek sportster. With its racer-style appearance, incredible performance for the time and sweet handling, it was one of the most exciting street bikes of its era.
As the American magazine *Cycle Rider*

discovered, a stock Z1 could be converted into a Rickman Metisse in just 6½ working hours. All you needed to put this beauty together was a Z1 engine, carbs, air filter, exhaust system, centre and side stands, battery compartment, instruments, cables, control levers and electrics. The rest was all Rickman... including the famous nickel-plated racing frame and faultless glassware.

Right: Several Rickman Z1s were raced, including the SS Performance-tuned model entered by Thruxton Motor Cycles of Andover, Hampshire. In racing trim, maximum speed was boosted to almost 145mph. Special features of this machine included triple Lockheed disc brakes, five-spoke cast-alloy wheels, Dunlop racing tyres, larger bore carbs and reversed Girling rear shocks.

Below: Street version of the Rickman Z1 racer. Except for the addition of direction indicators, air-filtration system, silencer instead of open megaphone for four-into-one exhaust, and a dual seat, the two versions were virtually identical.

Opposite page: Rickman offered its customers a variety of options — for example, a touring fairing, sports fairing, single or dual seat. Photograph shows tank outer cover, inner steel tank (for British market), glassfibre seat base, single seat pad. Note also the fitment of engine protection bars on this particular machine, just one item from Rickman's comprehensive accessory catalogue.

Above: Ultimate Rickman roadburner, the 1979 Metisse Z1000 Turbocharger (1015cc, 70x66mm) on the company's stand at the Earls Court Show that year. Even in road trim, it was capable of staggering performance: 150mph maximum and the standing quarter in under 10 seconds. Unfortunately, the recession and consequent sharp downturn in demand meant that this was to prove one of the last of the Rickman Metisse street bikes.

Opposite page:
The first Van Veen Wankel was this development machine produced in 1972. It was constructed as a mobile test bed for the OCR1000 project. This initial machine was powered by a converted twin-rotor Japanese Mazda car engine with a capacity of 491cc per chamber, housed in a modified and lengthened Moto Guzzi V7 frame. Claimed power output was in the region of 100bhp at 7,000rpm, with maximum torque developed at 4,000rpm. Registered by Van Veen as 'Hell on Wheels', the bike had a Guzzi clutch, gearbox and shaft drive. Despite the size of the Mazda car engine, width was not excessive. Widest points were the radiator, mounted ahead of the front down tube, and the oil cooler, just in front of the rider's knees.

Backroom boy behind the Van Veen Superbike was a young German engineer, Hans-Jurgen Klusowski. Originally from Kassel, Klusowski had first hit the headlines in 1970 when he built one of the world's first Wankel-engined motorcycles, using a BMW rolling chassis and the engine from an NSU Spyder car.

VAN VEEN

The Dutch-based Van Veen organisation is famous on two accounts: firstly for its World Championship-winning 50cc Kreidler racers, and secondly for the development and limited production of the fabulous OCR1000 Wankel-engined Superbike. This might seem strange, as the two machines are at directly opposite ends of the two-wheel world. But the Van Veen team, using mostly the same engineers, successfully developed both designs.

The Wankel engine has an interesting and complex history, arising initially from the efforts of the gifted German engineer, Felix Wankel, who had been experimenting during the Second World War with rotary-valve discs for torpedo engines. Later, Dr. Wankel applied his knowledge to a simple supercharger-compressor which enabled an NSU moped engine to propel a record-breaking streamliner to 121.9mph — all on only 50cc! The head of research at NSU, Dip. Ing. Walter Froede, realised that by applying the principles of combustion to this compressor, a source of pure rotary power could be achieved.

In truth, the only thing 'rotary' about the Wankel engine is its combustion process, which takes places in a chamber known as the epitrochoidal chamber, within which a rotor rotates eccentrically. The 'rotary piston', which is a rounded equilateral triangle shape, is connected to the central power shaft by gearing and is supported on eccentric bearings which allow it to rotate while keeping its three tips in contact with the epitrochoid chamber. Gas-sealing tips are provided at the tips of the rotor — a feature which gave considerable trouble on some early engines, most notably the ill-fated NSU RO80 car. Modern Wankels, including the production Van Veen OCR1000 use ceramic technology for sealing the rotors and chambers.

With the rotor-tip sealing problem largely overcome, the Wankel's only drawback is its high fuel consumption. Its advantages are many, including a smooth delivery of power, and are perhaps most graphically demonstrated on the Mazda RX7 sports car, now an acknowledged modern-era classic.

Other than the Van Veen creation, the only Wankel-engined motorcycles to have reached full production have been the Hercules (DKW) W2000, the Suzuki RE5 and the Norton Rotary. But only the Dutch machine has been in the true Superbike category, at least in engine size.

Left: The OCR1000 twin-rotor engine had a 996cc chamber volume and produced in excess of 100bhp, giving the 295kg (650lb) monster a top speeed of 130mph and, for its weight, staggering acceleration. With considerable technical assistance from Audi/NSU (part of the giant Volkswagen group), the engines were produced by Comotor of Luxembourg at their Altforweiler factory, near Saarbrucken.

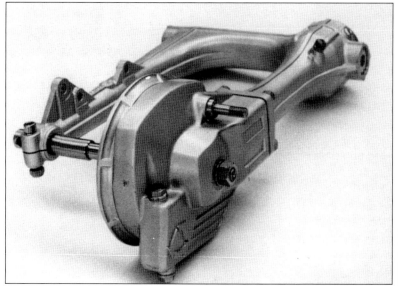

Left: The final drive assembly and swinging arm were designed, together with the gearbox unit, by Porsche engineers.

Below: The view most got of an OCR1000 is shown in this picture from the 1976 Amsterdam Show. Silencers on this example are in polished stainless steel.

Previous page, top:
The production version of the OCR1000 did not appear until some four years later, in 1976. Intended from the outset as a luxury superbike, with a limited market, the machine was totally hand-built around its twin-rotor engine. Much of the OCR1000 was manufactured with assistance from various German companies including Audi/NSU and Porsche. The frame of the Van Veen giant was designed by Jaap Voskamp of Kreidler racing fame. The triple-disc brake setup was Brembo, while the front and rear suspension were of Koni manufacture. The machine was equipped with a 21.5-litre (4.75 imp. gallon) tank, which was needed as consumption was well under 30mpg if the OCR's full performance was unleashed.

DRESDA

Dave Degens is a survivor. He began racing and then building motorcycles 30 years ago and is still thriving.

From racing in the early 1960s, Degens progressed to building Tritons for the café racer era (see the companion to this book, *Café Racers of the 1960s*), to short circuit racing, to winning the Barcelona 24-Hour Race (in 1965 and 1970), and then into a new era with Japanese-powered specials during the 1970s, when his success in the Barcelona marathon led to the Paris-based Japauto concern asking him to build an endurance racer around the four-cylinder 750/900 Honda engine.

In 1972 this collaboration resulted in the famous Bol d'Or win by the pairing of Debrock and Ruiz riding a 969cc Japauto housed in a Dresda chassis and weighing only 170kg (375lb). This success was repeated in 1973 against a vast array of works opposition: quite some achievement, and one which firmly established the Dresda name.

Today, the continuing enthusiasm for classic machinery, together with a fresh interest in his first creation, the Triton, ensure that Dave Degens' talents remain in demand.

Left: Constructed in small numbers during the early 1970s, the Dresda Suzuki T500 used the simple 493cc (70x64mm) piston-port twin-cylinder engine. This robust unit produced 47bhp at 7,000rpm in standard form, but as racing examples had proved this could be upped considerably with tuning. Almost everything about the machine was 'special'. For a start, it employed the Dresda front brake — a formidable stopper manufactured in magnesium. On the T500 this was of the 2LS variety, not the double-sided four leading shoe example seen on the Dresda Triumph-engined endurance racers. The frame, forks (Italian Ceriani) and swinging arm were all of the type able to provide superb bend-swinging abilities. Girling rear shocks, a conical rear hub, alloy rims, special silencers, racing tank, seat and fairing, together with Dunlop TT100 tyres, completed the picture.

Above: Another Dresda Suzuki venture was the GT750 three-cylinder watercooled super sports roadster. Unlike the smaller Dresda Suzuki, the 750 employed the original Japanese frame, forks and wheels, the only changes being a square section swinging arm, alloy rims, Dunlop tyres, and the usual café racer styling including tank, seat, revised side panels, deletion of airbox and filtering system (instead using simple open bellmouths), and fitted clip-ons and rearsets. Dave Degens is pictured above preparing to test the original prototype… and is seen overleaf testing its bend-swinging abilities on the open road.

Below: The 1973 Seeley Suzuki T500 Daytona racer, ridden at Brands Hatch that year by Pat Mahoney, was an attempt to make the most of power-to-weight ratios with monocoque construction which had long been employed in the aviation industry and in motor racing.

Early developments appeared with the Ossa 250 GP racer and Eric Offenstadt's Kawasaki, followed in the early 1970s by the John Player Norton.

The engine was chosen as it was readily available as a complete package, already proved competitive and reliable. A two-stroke was better suited to this type of chassis, because of its low height and compact form. Designed by Bob Cakebread and Les Apps, the material used for the frame was NS4 which has high strength characteristics, carrying a steel headstock and swing-arm mounting. The box section drew its strength from internal ribs and webs, and the assembly was riveted together, avoiding distortion and facilitating repair and/or modification. The advantages gained were increased rigidity and lighter weight. It also incorporated all the cycle parts in one unit, thus reducing build costs. The engine was rubber-mounted, with special cast-alloy wheels with twin discs at the front and a single at the rear. The discs were something of an innovation in that they were alloy, which was rough machined and then flame-sprayed with a special bronze material before final machining. Although the Seeley monocoque was not to go beyond the prototype stage, it did bring the concept of power-to-weight ratio to the attention of the public.

SEELEY

Colin Seeley was a sidecar racer of considerable repute during the 1960s, first with British-powered AMC-engined machinery and finally a Rennsport BMW outfit.

In 1965, Seeley made the business decision which was to shape his future when he purchased the rights to build AMC's racers — AJS 7R, Matchless G50 and Manx Norton (the Norton side was eventually sold off to John Tickle). This led to the construction of several interesting machines, and not just those using AMC power units, as Seeley had at an early stage decided to update the 7R and G50 with the addition of his own special frame assembly. As the Seeley enterprise was into limited production, with high quality engineering, it was also able to use its own brakes and many other components, as well as the basic engine, gearbox and clutch.

Many engine types were eventually to find their way into Seeley chassis, the most notable being the QUB (Queens University, Belfast) two-strokes of Dr Gordon Blair, the Suzuki T500 twin and a whole succession of Honda units including a 200 single (for trials) and various four-cylinder units for fast road work.

Recently, Colin Seeley played a vital part in the Brabham Formula 1 racing team, where his leadership and engineering skills were highly valued. He has had connections with Brabham since the early 1970s. He also helped run the 1993 Duckham Oils Crighton Norton Rotary team with Jim Moodie as rider in major British short circuit events.

Below: The first real update for the CB750 came in 1975 with the 750F (67bhp at 8,500rpm), featuring revised (Euro) styling. This is the Seeley version, basically much as before but with cosmetic revisions. Four-into-one exhaust is standard 750F Honda issue. Biggest advantage of the Seeley 750F over the stock version was its greatly improved handling and roadholding.

Previous page: Two versions of the Seeley Honda CB750 four-cylinder Superbike of the mid-1970s. The first is the base model with standard 738cc (61x63mm) single overhead cam engine, exhaust, front end (less wheel), plus Seeley-made alloy tank and dual racing seat, cast-alloy wheels, Avon tyres and Girling rear shocks.

The 'hot' version had an 812cc Dixon-Yoshimura conversion, extra tuning, bigger carbs with no air filters, four-into-one exhaust, rear disc brake, lightweight wheels, Michelin tyres, clip-ons, single racing seat in alloy, and a tank in the same material. Both machines had the Seeley-Honda frame and swinging-arm assembly manufactured in Reynolds 531 tubing.

Overleaf: Interesting Seeley Honda 1000 of 1977 — still with sohc. Big bore kits were available from the likes of Yoshimura and Action Four. To cope with additional performance (around 85bhp and 135mph, compared with 67bhp and 115mph in the 'cooking' sohc CB750), braking had been uprated by an additional disc up front. Another major change was the new and less restrictive silencer for the four-into-one system.

(Note also Rickman Honda in background. Both these Superbike Specials offered enthusiasts extra 'go' and superior bend-swinging abilities, at extra cost over the stock bike.)

Below: After Phil Read won the 1977 Formula 1 TT, Honda in conjunction with the Seeley organisation offered this 'Phil Read Replica' through the British dealer network. Production was limited and sales were usually to special order only. Overall, it was very much a case of the standard CB750 F2 four-cylinder model being offered with a new set of clothes, rather than of any radical changes in chassis or engine. Wheels were standard Honda Comstar assemblies of the era. Compared with the earlier 750F, the F2 engine gave 70bhp at 9,500rpm, this being achieved by the installation of bigger valves and the fitting of a higher lift cam. Inlet valve sizes increased from 32 to 34mm, exhausts from 28 to 31mm, with stiffer valve springs completing the picture.

Opposite page :
The Honda Britain livery of 1979 seen at the Earls Court Show in November that year — with additional glamour. By now it was available in both 750 and 900 engine sizes, using the latest dohc engine type. As with the Phil Read Replica, it was very much a sheep in wolf's clothing.

Above: Model Linda Frost is seen here on the 1200TTS Münch Mammoth, star of the Racing and Sporting Show, London, which opened on January 2, 1970. This was the era of the collaboration involving sidecar racer/builder Helmut Fath, his partner Dr Peter Kuhn, George Bell and Münch. The latest version of the Mammoth had a capacity of 1177cc and a reputed power out put of 90bhp.

One of the first projects for the new team was an even larger capacity version of the Münch four which was built to attack the world one-hour land speed record held by Mike Hailwood on an MV 500 four, at 145mph for the 60 minutes. Constructed in just six weeks, the new machine

was also intended to provide valuable publicity for the Münch street bikes. As Bell was from Florida, what better place to flaunt this machine than Daytona? — and so the 'Daytona Bomb' was born. The engine from the 1200TTS roadster was bored out to 1370cc and produced a mind-blowing 125bhp at 8,600rpm. Specially cast alloy cylinders replaced the original's cast-iron components. Drive to the camshaft was, as on the standard engine, by duplex chain up the nearside of the engine. The high dome 13:1 pistons necessitated the use of a set of powered rollers to start the brute. Carburation was taken care of by a quartet of 35mm Dell'Orto SSI racing instruments, with each pair sharing a remotely fitting flat chamber.

MÜNCH

The first Münch Mammoth was built for a French customer in the winter of 1965-66. It used a tuned version of the recently released NSU Prinz 1000TT 1085cc car engine housed in a one-off set of cycle parts, many of which were made by Friedl Münch himself in his small Friedberg workshop.

Before delivery, it was comprehensively tested by the respected journalist Ernst Leverkus (father of the famous Elephant Rally) for *Das Motorrad* magazine. And it was Leverkus who really told the world about Münch and his machine.

Leverkus was enthusiastic not only about the Mammoth's 125mph maximum speed (confirmed at Hockenheim race circuit), but also about the machine's ability to travel all day on the autobahn at 110mph with a level of comfort and sheer muscle which easily surpassed any of its contemporaries.

After its public launch at the Cologne Show in September 1966, a new modified version of the Münch appeared, with engine capacity upped to 1177cc and improved performance. It attracted the attention of the millionaire American publisher Floyd Clymer, leading to a business partnership which lasted until just before Clymer's untimely death in the spring of 1970 and a brand new factory facility at Ossenheim.

Thereafter a succession of business partners appeared on the scene, including another American, George Bell, and Heinz W. Henke, which allowed Münch to develop the Mammoth throughout much of the 1970s, albeit on a 'stop-go' basis.

Right: On the 'Daytona Bomb' (standard engine shown here), lubrication was by a semi-dry sump system as the crankshaft was not submerged in oil. To cope with such extra demands, a larger capacity system was employed where the lubricant was contained in a separate magnesium sump bolted to the underside of the engine. The flywheel was removed, which left the five-bearing crankshaft to be dynamically balanced after the primary drive pinion was fitted. This was driven by specially-made helical gears on the nearside of the engine which in turn drove the standard Münch four-speed gearbox via a 12-plate dry clutch. To cope with the much greater power output, the clutch was considerably enlarged.

An additional 10mm spark plug was provided for each cylinder. The original 14mm plugs were activated by a Volkswagen distributor which sat in front of the engine and was driven by a single-row chain with a tensioner pulley on the right-hand end of the crankshaft. The second set of plugs had their own distributor. This was mounted on the right-hand end of the camshaft with 38 degrees advance being employed.

Above: After waiting for the end of the annual Cycle Week at Daytona in March 1970, the Münch team was delayed first by the weather and subsequently by tyre problems…

When the record runs finally got under way, the 'Daytona Bomb' rocketed through the electronic eye at 178mph on the Daytona banking. That it was unable to sustain this performance was due not to lack of reliability in the mechanical components, but to the tyres, which saw rear tread disappear after no more than three laps — about nine miles. Even changing tyre compounds didn't help: the brutal fact of the matter was that in 1970 the motorcycle tyre didn't exist which was able to meet the demands of the 1400cc behemoth.

The motorcycle was stored in a Miami warehouse where it languished for eleven years before a court order awarded it to one of its American backers, in lieu of payments owed. In Europe, limited production of the street bike continued; one of them is pictured here at the Cologne Show in September 1970.

Right: By 1972, ownership of the Münch name had passed to a new backer: Hassia GmbH, a packaging company with branches throughout Germany. Hassia's expansion programme for the Münch roadsters involved not only increasing production of the Mammoth, but also developing a new three-cylinder two-stroke. This latter machine — pictured here at the 1972 Cologne Show — had a capacity of 660cc and the separate air-cooled cylinders and heads were set transversely across the frame. Several engine components came from a Sachs snowmobile unit. Almost the only feature the newcomer shared with its big brother was the front brake, otherwise everything was new. The frame was a neat full double cradle with exposed Ceriani-type front forks plus rear shocks with exposed chrome multi-rate springs. The legend 'Münch 3' was emblazoned upon the sides of the 20-litre fuel tank. No production examples were ever offered for sale.

Below: Besides publicly displaying the prototype three-cylinder model for the first time, Münch also showed a sports version of the 1200TTS. This featured additional tuning — power increased to almost 100bhp — ace 'bars, a new exhaust system with four separate megaphones finished in matt black, a new combined rear mudguard and dual racing-style seat, larger capacity fuel tank, larger 180mm headlamp, Nippo Denso instruments and a wider section rear tyre.

Left: Yet another financial backer appeared at the end of 1973, after the whole Hassia organisation went bankrupt. This was Heinz Henke, who became interested after hearing of Münch's financial problems while having his own 1200 TTS serviced! Henke purchased the remains of the company after it went into liquidation at a knockdown price. The new Heinz Henke company, as it was now named, was based in a small, modern factory unit at Waldsiedlung, a few kilometres north-east of Altenstadt. When production restarted in the spring of 1974, it was concentrated at first on just two models, both of which used the 1177cc NSU-based four-cylinder engine with a bore and stroke of 75x66.6mm.

Below: The top-of-the-line 4TTS/E (illustrated) had a compression ratio of 8.5:1 and generated 104bhp at 7,500rpm with Bosch fuel injection. The cheaper 4TTS had two twin choke Weber carburettors and a lower power output of 88bhp at 7,000rpm. The only immediately visible difference between the two models was the seating. The 4TTS/E featured a single racing-style saddle, while the 4TTS came with a dual seat as standard. Both models had several common points in their technical specification, including gear ratios — 1st 2.53:1, 2nd 1.55:1, 3rd 1.14:1 and 4th 1:1 — the ⅝" x ⅜" heavy-duty final drive chain, 34-litre capacity fuel tank, and

12-volt electrical system with 180 watt alternator. In the mid-1970s, just as Henke's policies were beginning to be vindicated by the company's new-found stability, Friedl Münch decided that Henke's good business sense was actually restricting his own creative flair and stifling new development. Early in 1977, the two men went their separate ways. Henke continued production of the TTS and TTS/E until the recession of the early 1980s brought about their decline and ultimate end, while Münch continued building the occasional one-off and offering big-bore kits for existing owners giving either 1400 or 1500cc, as a separate operation.

GUS KUHN

In 1968 the long-established Gus Kuhn business in Stockwell, London, was transformed almost overnight. The car agency business was dropped and stocks were cleared out. In their place appeared rows of gleaming new Nortons, BSAs and Triumphs. A thrusting customising service for Nortons was set up.

And the Gus Kuhn équipe went racing in a big way, with 750cc Norton Commandos in production machine events and 350cc and 500cc Seeleys in the racing classes. By the end of the 1968 season, Dave Croxford, on a Kuhn Seeley, was the new British 500cc champion. He retained the championship the following year.

On Kuhn Seeleys and Commandos, Mick Andrews became the 'find' of British racing in 1969. His many superb performances included a tremendous victory in the international Hutchinson 100 production machine race.

The man behind all this activity was Vincent (Dave) Davey, who before joining Gus Kuhn in 1950 had served his time at both Norton and BSA. Three years later he became a director, and he and his wife, Marian, inherited the business when Marian's father Gus died in 1966.

Vincent Davey had always been interested in racing. In the early 1950s he had ridden a 250 Rudge and a 500 Norton, before retiring from the racing scene to devote all his energies to business. Under his leadership, the Gus Kuhn empire grew in the 1970s, not only to continue its Norton Commando business, but also to become the British importer for MV Agusta (1972-1974) and to develop a major BMW franchise, which in the 1980s was to become its sole source of revenue.

The 1970 Gus Kuhn Shell-backed racing team. Left to right: Vincent Davey (Team Manager), Dave Sleat (mechanic), Frank Kateley (mechanic), Mick Andrew (rider), Tom Dickie (rider), Mrs Davey and daughter Valerie, Charlie Sanby (rider) and Pat Mahoney (rider). Machines are all Seeley framed, with either 500 G50 single-cylinder or 750 Commando engines.

Below: Another rider to achieve race-winning performances on Gus Kuhn machinery was Ron Whittich (seen here with glasses). He won numerous victories on Kuhn Commandos such as the one pictured here at Snetterton in 1971. Note optional 'extra' double-disc front brakes and raised silencers to provide superior ground clearance.

Opposite page:
Front page of the extensive 1971 Gus Kuhn Norton catalogue. Motorcycle is street version of the Kuhn Commando, with boss Vincent Davey in the saddle. A very British bulldog — the team's mascot — keeps a close eye on the cameraman.

Below: Just some of the tuning goodies from the 1971 Kuhn Norton catalogue. These include Commando and Atlas pistons in 9 or 10:1 ratios, cylinder head steady assembly, various oversize valves, Commando Nimonic 80A polished exhaust valve, oversize valve guides, phosphar bronze valve guides, Commando and Atlas valve springs, Norton twin-cylinder engine tappets (cam followers), Commando camshaft, Gus Kuhn engine timing disc, engine sprocket and clutch withdrawal tool, half time pinion withdrawal tool, Champion N6Y spark plug, clutch withdrawal tool, strobe timing light, Amal 930 and 932 Concentric Mark 1 carburettors, Gardner 32mm carburettor, carburettor air intake (velocity stack) in varying sizes.

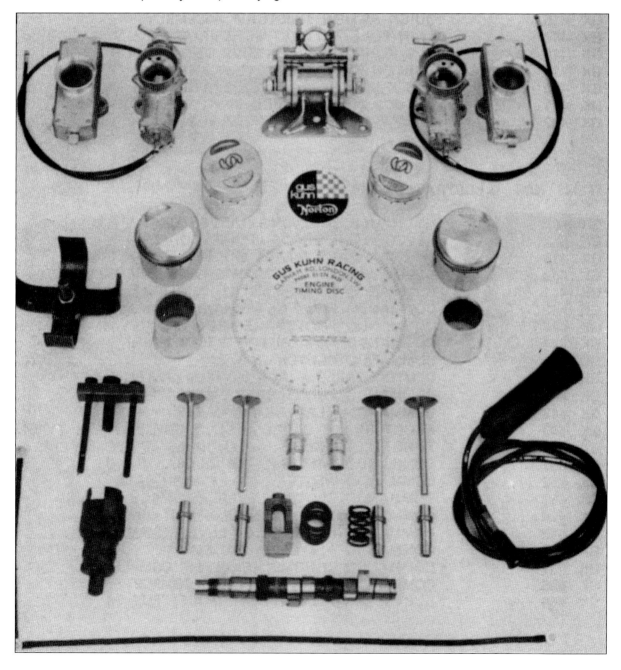

Above: The 1972 Gus Kuhn F750 Commando-based short circuit racer. Features include front and rear disc brakes, Seeley-type chassis, alloy rims, clip-ons with Tommaselli controls, hi-level exhaust system, tuned engine, Dural rear wheel sprocket, glassfibre tank, seat fairing and front mudguard, alloy central oil tank, choice of Krober electronic or Smiths mechanically operated tacho, dry clutch and close ratio gears.

Above: One of the special Gus Kuhn BMW flat-twins used in long-distance racing at events such as the Bol d'Or and Barcelona 24 Hours in the mid-to-late 1970s. Riders included John Cowie and Martin Sharpe. Gus Kuhn also went racing with MV Agustas, though less effectively than with German or British models.

Below: Three new Gus Kuhn 750 Commandos for the 1972 season. Left to right: Super Sports (priced £712), Sports (£625) and Tourer (£696). *Motor Cycle* achieved a highest one-way speed of 121mph when road-testing the Super Sport.

Above: The year 1974 saw Anelli replaced by Guiseppe Elementi as official rider for the Rimini-based outfit. And it was Elementi who was to be the first rider to win Bimota international acclaim with a series of outstanding results on the Bimota-framed Yamaha two-stroke twin. Elementi won many races in Italy that year and achieved an excellent seventh place in the Italian Grand Prix at Imola. Clearly the racing connection was a vitally important factor in Bimota's evolution, with a further major boost coming in 1975 when Johnny Cecotto took the 350cc world title on another Bimota-framed Yamaha. These achievements brought in enormous publicity and a corresponding increase in orders.

Left: Demand for a roadgoing replica of Bimota's original Honda 750 led in 1974 to the appearance of the HB1 (Honda Bimota 1). Like Anelli's earlier racer, this too used a CB750 engine. However, the main intention of Bimota in those early days was to supply frame kits rather than complete machines.

BIMOTA

The Bimota marque was born more by accident than design, though for superbike enthusiasts the accident was a singularly happy one.

Massimo Tamburini owned a heating business in the town of Rimini, on the Adriatic coast, an area which had long been a centre for both racing and building motorcycles. As a hobby, Tamburini modified several of the local riders' machines to make them not only quicker, but also lighter and better-handling. His efforts were rewarded with success, and before very long his work on one particular machine, an MV Agusta 600 four, was gaining the admiration of the entire national motorcycle fraternity.

But it was an event in the summer of 1972 which was the real key to the creation of the Bimota company. The event was a routine test session at Misano race circuit where Tamburini, his friend Giuseppe Morri and racer Luigi Anelli were testing a special-framed Honda 750 four. A journalist who was present wrote an article about Tamburini's Honda, creating such a wave of interest that a commercial organisation was established to meet the consequent influx of orders. The company took its name from the three partners who set it up: *Bi*anchi, *Mo*rri and *Ta*mburini.

The new venture began trading on January 1, 1973. In addition to the Honda 750, Tamburini had just finished building a pukka racing machine powered by one of the rapid Yamaha TR2 motors. The prototype of this machine, with Luigi Anelli in the saddle, made its debut at Modena, early in 1973, and it soon became clear that Bimota had something special on their hands.

Just how special was to become apparent over the next few years, with a succession of both racing and street motorcycles which had few equals.

Right: The Bimota drawing office, photographed in late 1975. Even though the HB1 was a sales success, the racing programme came first at that time. The major reason for this was Bimota's ability to construct one-off frames as well as larger batches for series production. At that time the roadgoing Bimota was still in its infancy and the company's revenue came mainly from the racing fraternity.

Not until 1976, and then purely by chance, did Bimota offer their first production roadsters as a complete package. This came about through their connection with Suzuki-Italia. As a joint venture, Bimota had constructed a batch of 50 SB1s — a combination of a Bimota chassis and Suzuki's T500 two-stroke twin engine. Although a 'racing only' venture, it was so successful that Suzuki-Italia came back with an order for 200 GS750-powered superbikes, this time for street rather than track use.

Left: SB2. The first glimpse the public had of this sensational-looking projectile came at the Bologna Show in January 1977. To enable Bimota to meet initial orders, the workforce was increased from 16 to 30. It was reported at the time that Suzuki technicians had flown in from Japan especially to look at the new bike, and give their approval, before the show opened.

The S2 was nothing if not unorthodox. The four-gallon fuel tank was mounted *under* the engine, with an electric pump to lift fuel to carburettor height. The tank placing lowered the centre of gravity by some 14 percent compared to the conventional Suzuki GS750. In the performance stakes, the Bimota was capable of a stunning 143mph — more than 20mph quicker than the GS750 which shared the same power unit. This was due mainly to efficient streamlining and the SB2's lighter 180kg (396lb) weight.

Below: The steering-column of the SB2 was inclined at 25 degrees to achieve not only greater manoeuvreability but also greater sensitivity for the rider. The 35mm Ceriani racing-type forks were inclined at 29 degrees to improve roadholding qualities over fast sections and to hold down the rear of the bike during hard braking.

Both the frame and the square section swinging arm were made from chrome-moly tubing. Setting a trend was the single, vertically mounted De Carbon racing car-type monoshock suspension unit. By current standards, the respective weights of the frame and swinging arm of 8.6kg (19lb) and 3.4 kg (7.5lb) were extremely light. Much of the development in this area was later to be seen on the new breed of Japanese machines which emerged in the 1980s.

Above: The next development in the evolution of the Bimota
Superbike appeared at the 1977 Milan Show. Once again, Massimo
Tamburini had produced a mouth-watering cocktail of technology and
flamboyant styling. The newcomer was the KB1, housing either a
Kawasaki 903cc (66x66mm) or 1015cc (70x66mm) dohc four. The
KB1 made full use of three key Bimota features which the company
had proved in its line of racing chassis: variable steering geometry,
space frame, and monoshock rear suspension.

Variable steering geometry was a Bimota exclusive. As with the SB2,
the fork legs (now 38mm) and steering column were at slightly
different angles. By featuring eccentric upper and lower steering-head
bearings, the trail could be changed to suit the rider's requirements
for either fast or twisty conditions. The KB1 steering column was
inclined at 24 degrees and the fork legs at 28 degrees, while the trail
could be varied between 3.9 and 4.7 inches.

Unlike the Suzuki frame, the Kawasaki's did not feature the 'split'
design of the main side tubes. This was because on the Kawasaki the
engine was mounted that much higher. Another major difference was
that the single rear suspension unit was now mounted horizontally.

Above: In 1977, together with his son Giovanni, Magni founded *Elaborazioni Magni di Magni Giovanni*. The new company not only continued to offer specialised MV Agusta parts and services, but commenced production and sale of cast alloy and drum brake wheels. Father and son are pictured here with a small selection of their wares.

Left: Other MV components followed, two of the most important being a special frame and a chain-drive conversion kit. The latter was unquestionably the most popular of the Magni MV extras. Not only did it benefit performance, but it also assisted reliability by eliminating the problems associated with the original equipment drive shaft assembly.

MAGNI

Below: The Magni frame kit had its origins in a similar dissatisfaction with the standard product. This example, belonging to Northamptonshire enthusiast Richard Marchant, has many of the Magni extras including the frame, Forcella Italia (formerly Ceriani) front forks, Magni tank and seat, and the racing exhaust system. The engine has an 862cc conversion plus paired cylinder barrels, ported heads, 30mm carbs, electronic ignition, special cams, chain-drive conversion and other goodies. It also goes like the wind, as the author discovered for himself during several laps around Cadwell Park in the early 1980s.

For over a quarter of a century, one man was the prime mover behind the fabulous success garnered by the MV Agusta équipe on the world's motorcycle racing circuits — and it wasn't the legendary Count!

In appearance, the stocky bespectacled Arturo Magni was typically Italian. In manner, however, he was quite the reverse of his voluble, often excitable countrymen. On those rare occasions when he deemed it necessary to talk at all, Magni chose his words carefully and used as few of them as possible.

As a motorcycle team manager and tactician, and above all as a 'company man', Magni's quiet diplomacy stood him in good stead; indeed, it must have been at least part of the reason for his long period at the very top of the tree. In achievement, he ranks as the motorcycle racing world's equivalent of the legendary Alfred Neubauer, of Mercedes-Benz fame.

Magni joined MV Agusta in 1950 and stayed with them until the mid-1970s, when the famous marque withdrew from the sport. Still as deeply committed as ever, he then turned his skills to producing a wide range of special equipment and tuning parts for the roadgoing MV fours.

Previous pages:
The Magni MV frame was manufactured from lightweight chrome-moly
tubing with a strengthened headstock. Its twin top tubes ran so close to
the inlet cover that the engine had to be removed from the frame in
order to adjust the valves; but, as on the racer, the engine could be slid
out sideways after removal of the offside downtube and bottom rail,
fixed by six bolts. The swinging arm was of box-section tubing,
although there were two quite different designs. The first used plain
Teflon bushes and the rear spindle was carried on an eccentric
mounting to allow chain adjustment without disturbing wheel alignment
— although to avoid handling problems the spindle could not be
adjusted above the centre line of the swinging arm. This version was
manufactured by Bimota, whose name was stamped on the adjusters.
The alternative arrangement used taper roller bearings and carried the
wheel spindle in sliding blocks with drawbolt and locknut adjusters.

Above: Magni also offered cylinder conversions, first of 837cc and
later 862cc. Both used paired barrels, rather than the four separate
ones favoured by the factory, and where the factory castings had 11
fins, both Magni conversions had only nine, with a much coarser
finish to the alloy. Magni barrels had to be set up with a richer
mixture for the two inner cylinders than was used for the production
MV fours.

Above: Another Magni modification on offer was an electronic ignition conversion, made by Marelli and identical to that fitted to the Alfasud Ti 1.3 and later Fiat 132 cars. Customers could purchase high-lift (9.5mm) camshafts and 30 or 32mm Dell'Orto PHF pumper carbs, as well as curved racing-style pipes and silencers. Fitting this exhaust system was a more complex task than might have been immediately apparent: it could easily take a whole day, as the pipes ran very close to the frame and often required tailoring to ensure a good fit. This particular version, using an 837cc conversion, tank, seat side panels, electronic ignition and exhaust system, was built by John Lee, of Verghera Engineering, Suffolk.

SPECIAL SPECIALS

uch as the giants of the motorcycle industry might wish to deny it, many of the most interesting and innovative machines have been the products of small engineering workshops or even of single-minded enthusiasts constructing their own home-built specials in a garage or garden shed.

For proof of this phenomenon, one only has to look at the vast number of one-off or limited-run hand-built motorcycles which have been built and ridden over the decades and have won their place in the history books. The small selection of seventies superbikes on the following pages bears its own testimony to that tradition.

Previous page

Top: Some two thousand working hours went into this 800cc special, built by a Dutch enthusiast in 1973. It was powered by a Honda four-cylinder car engine. Gearbox, wheel hubs and front forks were Norton…

Bottom: …The Tabia 800MTS, as it was christened, was a credit to its constructor. Note the neat installation of radiator and oil-cooler assemblies at the front of the engine, and the four separate exhaust pipes and silencers.

Below: Another Dutch-built special, this time using an 855cc four-cylinder engine constructed from a number of different sources: a Ford Anglia bottom half with NSU Prinz cylinders, Volvo pistons and Renault valves. A Matchless gearbox and home-made clutch were fitted. Frame was a combination of BMW and DKW components, while other features included Dell'Orto UBF carburettors and a Velocette front hub.

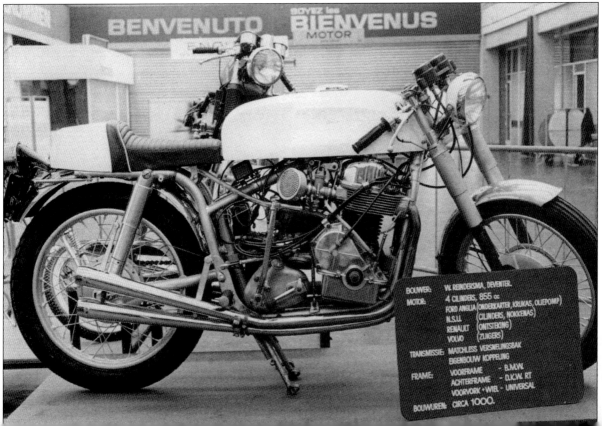

Previous page: The Hultink-NSU (Hultinsu) was a Dutch alternative to the Münch Mammoth, with its mighty 1200 NSU car engine shoe-horned into the long-suffering Norton Featherbed frame. Front wheel was genuine Manx Norton, with a disc at the rear.

Left: Close up of the Hultinsu showing Manx alloy tanks, rear chain enclosure, tacho drive from cylinder head. Norton gearbox and Laverda clutch are hidden beneath the specially fabricated outer engine cover.

Below: A specially constructed Moto Guzzi V7 Sport *circa* 1974, with glassfibre tank and seat, non-standard cast-alloy front wheel, stock rear drum. Other interesting features are two-into-one exhaust with single open matt black megaphone, massive 38mm Dell'Orto pumper carbs, cylinder head guards and Koni rear shocks. Maximum power 70bhp, maximum speed 130mph.

Above: An eye-catcher at the 1974 Isle of Man TT was this Suzuki
— a watercooled 500. But this was no factory prototype — it had
been made by Barton Motors, of South Wales.

Terry Hart, the man behind the project, rode the machine from
Caernarvon to Liverpool and used the TT period to get in some
miles on the bike, which was completed only hours before his
departure for the island. Basically the machine was a 380 Suzuki
triple. But the cylinder block was replaced by a Barton watercooled
block with larger cylinder bores (61 instead of 52mm) which, using
the standard 54mm stroke, gave a capacity of 472cc. Carburettors
were 28mm Mikunis and compression ratio was 6.8:1. It would
have cost very little more than the standard aircooled GT550 of the
time, but with the advantages of a six-speed gearbox and
watercooling.

Sadly, the factory never adopted Hart's design — it was very much
a case of a good idea going to waste. Later, Hart became the chief
engine designer for Armstrong, who built several race-winning
250cc track mounts in the early 1980s.

One of several Laverda three-cylinder superbikes built by the Croydon-based Motodd concern. This one was registered in 1979, at which time Motodd was run by longtime Laverda enthusiast Phil Todd. Most of the Motodd specials were powered by the 1000cc Jota engine. Changes from standard included frame, swinging arm, fork brace, wheels, exhaust, tank, side panels, mudguards, foot controls and pedals. Customers also had the option of availing themselves of Motodd's extensive tuning facilities, including a dyno.

Left: One of the many turbocharged Kawasaki fours to appear during the decade. A standard aircooled Z1000 of the late 1970s was capable of accelerating from zero to 60mph in a fraction over four seconds. With a turbo and very little else fitted, a one-litre Kawasaki four could achieve 60mph in *two seconds*, 100mph in five seconds, and 150mph in 10! Modifications needed to go with the turbo were a stronger cam chain, a welded crankshaft — to prevent twisting — and forged pistons. Compression ratio, when the turbocharger was boosting to 25lbs per square inch was around 13:1. Standard valves and ports could still be used, but with matching components and gas flowing. For serious competition use (drag racing), the standard clutch was adequate. Other changes usually included the removal of the starter motor, a Holley or similar fuel pump with a 110 gallon-per-hour capacitor, and electronic ignition.

The best examples put out some 170bhp — and the sight of one of them blasting off the startline was something to remember. The top Kawasaki turbos could achieve a quarter-mile terminal speed of almost 150mph.

Below: The weird 1979 Quasar… was it a motorcycle or was it a car? Well, actually, it was a combination of the two. Its power source was a Reliant four-cylinder 700cc ohv car engine, with a one-off frame giving a feet-forward riding stance. Motorcycle wheels, with Lockheed hydraulically operated disc brakes, Earles-type front forks, a streamlined glassfibre bodyshell, twin windscreen wiper blades, twin headlamps and an

offside-located fuel filler cap completed the specification.

Performance could not be described as anything but mundane, although lighter weight and superior streamlining made it significantly better than the Reliant original. Handling and roadholding were excellent — with the proviso that gale-force conditions were to be avoided at all times.

Previous page
Bottom: This one-off Benelli 750 Sei (747.77cc — 56x56.6mm), six-cylinder endurance racer was campaigned by the privateer MOC Equipe during the mid-1970s. Built by Benelli's French importer, Motobecane, the futuristic machine featured a specially commissioned chassis with a single horizontal rear shock. Intended for use in

the Prototypes category of events such as the Bol d'Or, the Motobecane-Benelli was capable of speeds up to 150mph. Of particular interest are the bolt-up split wheel rims and a rear sprocket that was *outboard* of the swinging arm. Other details were a fuel pump, a triangulated frame, quickly detachable fairing, tank and seat, Ceriani 38mm front forks and a De Carbon rear shock.

Renowned as one of Britain's leading authorities on motorcycle history and sport, **Mick Walker** is pictured above with his racing son Gary at Snetterton in March 1993. Machinery is a 1992 Suzuki RGV 250, modified for Super Sport 400 competition.